Old ELGIN

by
Iain Sinclair

To my dear wife Dorothy, for all her encouragement and patience while I wrote the text for th

In the days before foreign holidays, summer breaks featured much more 'at home' pleasures. This happy scene shows youngsters enjoying a dook in the River Lossie at a quiet spot between Bishopmill and the Haugh, which was a favourite place for a dip.

© Iain Sinclair 2000
First published in the United Kingdom, 2000,
by Stenlake Publishing Ltd.
54–58 Mill Square,
Catrine, Ayrshire KA5 6RD
Telephone: 01290 551122
www.stenlake.co.uk

ISBN 1 84033 128 3

The publishers regret that they cannot supply
copies of any pictures featured in this book.

The books listed below were used by the author during his research. None
of them are available from Stenlake Publishing. Those interested in finding
out more are advised to contact their local bookshop or reference library.

Historic Elgin and its Cathedral, Elgin Society, 1974.
Elgin Cathedral, Richard Fawcett, Historic Scotland.
Elgin Past and Present, Mike Seton, Moray District Libraries, 1980.
Moray Past and Present, Mike Seton, Moray District Libraries, 1978.
Elgin in Old Postcards, Mike Seton, 1983.
Churches of Moray, Angus Howat and Mike Seton, 1981.
Bridges in Moray, Alistair Scott, Moray Field Club, 1981.
Elgin Past and Present, H. B. Macintosh, 1914.

The village of Bishopmill, now incorporated into the town, was planned and laid out in the late eighteenth century. A new road linking Elgin and Lossiemouth was made through Bishopmill in 1821. This road created a cutting and the 'Dry Brig' (shown here) was constructed as a link over the road. The bridge became an obstacle to traffic and was destroyed in 1898.

INTRODUCTION

Lying some 70 miles north-west of Aberdeen and 35 miles east of Inverness, the Royal Burgh and City of Elgin is the principal town and administrative centre of Morayshire, and has enjoyed importance in the history of Scotland over the centuries. David I built a castle on top of Ladyhill, a natural defensive mound overlooking the town. By 1224 Elgin was important enough to be selected as the site for a new cathedral for the Bishopric of Moray, and prior to the Reformation this was the principal seat of learning north of Aberdeen, resulting in the title 'the lantern of the north'. During the period when Scotland was fighting with Edward II – 'the Hammer of the Scots' – the castle was reduced to a ruin. Not having any natural defences, Elgin fell prey to such people as Alexander Stewart, 'the Wolf of Badenoch', who plundered the town and cathedral in 1390, as did Alexander of the Isles in the early fifteenth century.

Despite these unwelcome visitors Elgin gradually grew and developed. The Reformation spelt the end of the cathedral which thereafter fell into ruin. This was probably hastened by the removal of the lead from its roof, which was shipped out of Aberdeen en route to Holland. Alas, the ship foundered not far from Aberdeen harbour and there are many who believed this was some form of divine judgement.

The town is blessed with some very fine buildings, and apart from the ruined cathedral (now in the care of Historic Scotland) there are impressive structures such as Dr Gray's Hospital, Anderson's Institute, St Giles Church and the Burgh Court Rooms (the latter were built in 1839 when the tolbooth, which stood in the High Street, became redundant). As Elgin grew in prosperity streets of fine houses – such as Duff Avenue and Forteath Avenue – began to be built for the merchants, lawyers and bankers of the town.

The coming of the railways enhanced the importance of Elgin, which became the place where lines from Aberdeen, Lossiemouth and the towns and villages to the south converged. In 1902 the gift of Grant Lodge and the surrounding 45 acres of ground to the town by Sir George Cooper paved the way for what is a splendid public park – Cooper Park. As people moved away from the cramped living conditions of the town centre, Elgin gradually expanded into what had formerly been separate villages – Bishopmill and New Elgin.

Many of the town's original trades have long since disappeared. The six incorporated trades of Elgin were represented by shoemakers, weavers, glovers, tailors, hammermen and square wrights. Today the town is more of an administrative centre and industry is mainly focused on food manufacture, weaving and whisky production. Elgin retains the atmosphere of a pleasant rural county town with a good quality of life and good facilities for education, health and recreation.

This 1903 photograph shows the staff of Elgin post office. In 1860 the post office moved into the Commercial Buildings in Commerce Street, then in 1884 it was transferred across the street to the premises shown here. These later became the offices of Johnston and Carmichael, chartered accountants, before they moved to South Street. The boys in the foreground were probably telegram boys, employed in large numbers to deliver messages before the days of faxes and e-mail. The post office was extended in 1909 and remained in Commerce Street until 1963 when it moved to purpose-built premises at the west end of High Street.

An unusual photograph of Elgin Cathedral, 'the lantern of the north', depicting the south corner of the east end of this magnificent ruin. The history of the cathedral goes back to 1224 when the then Pope gave his permission to locate a cathedral in Elgin. After a fire in 1270 the opportunity was taken to extend the building on a large scale and by the end of the thirteenth century it had reached its full size and included a chapter house on the north side of the choir as a meeting room for the canons. This chapter house has been fully restored in recent years and is used for wedding ceremonies. The cathedral was set on fire in 1390 by the notorious 'Wolf of Badenoch' who had a score to settle with the bishop. Repairs dragged on for over 100 years and had not been completed by the time of the Reformation, after which the building was pillaged for building materials. A gentleman by the name of John Shanks became the first keeper of the ruins in 1807 and, as recorded on his gravestone within the cathedral grounds, single-handedly cleared thousands of barrowloads of collapsed masonry to expose the remains of the once magnificent building. Today the cathedral is in the care of Historic Scotland who continue the work of preservation of the stonework and restoration of the towers at the west front.

Popularly known as the Bishop's Palace, this building is considered to be one of the finest specimens of fifteenth century domestic architecture in Scotland. Its origins probably date from around 1224 when the cathedral and college of canons were translated from nearby Spynie. The original building would have been quite small and probably became a more imposing structure about the beginning of the fifteenth century, when it would have made a more convenient residence for the bishop while the cathedral was being rebuilt after its destruction by the 'Wolf of Badenoch'. The south wing was said to have been added by Bishop Patrick Hepburn in 1557. The palace reverted to the Crown after the Reformation and was lived in by the Lord High Chancellor, the first Earl of Dunfermline until his death in 1622. About that time it became known as Dunfermline House. It was purchased by the Duke of Gordon in 1730 and was inhabited until the close of the eighteenth century when it was unroofed. Despite efforts to conserve the building in the late nineteenth century, the south wing collapsed in 1891. The building subsequently passed into the care of Historic Scotland under whose protection the remaining parts of it have been preserved.

The Panns Port or Water Gate. In medieval times Elgin had four main gates or ports through which people and traders coming into the town could be controlled. The gate remains intact to this day, and traces of the wall surrounding the cathedral are still visible at various points in the town.

The priory of Pluscarden was founded in 1230 by Alexander II for a French order – Vallus Caulian. 1454 saw the unification of Pluscarden and Urquhart priories and thereafter the former became a Benedictine priory. After the Reformation Pluscarden went into decline until it was virtually a ruin. It was acquired by the Marquis of Bute in 1943, and his son gifted it to the Benedictine monks of Prinknash. The first monks arrived in 1948 and since then an ambitious programme of rebuilding and expansion has gone on. 1974 saw the priory elevated to the status of an abbey, and today it attracts thousands of visitors from all over the world, drawn by the peace and beauty of the building and its surroundings.

W.R.&S. 23786. PLUSCARDEN PRIORY.

Looking towards the rooftops of Elgin from Morriston Farm, with its stooks of corn in the foreground. Prominent to the right is the column on Ladyhill. The dome of Dr Gray's Hospital can also be made out.

ELGIN FROM MORRISTON FARM

571

This photograph was taken from Ladyhill and looks over the rooftops of the houses in the lanes and closes leading off the High Street. The tower of St Giles Church dominates the skyline of the town centre. Developments over the years, particularly the building of the bypass, have meant major changes to this rooftop scene. To the right is the tower of Moss Street Church, now a café bar. The congregation of Moss Street Church amalgamated with the South Church in 1938.

Oldmills is the oldest mill on the banks of the Lossie. Its history probably goes back to 1230 when it was granted by Alexander II to the monks at Pluscarden as a meal mill. It has served other purposes over the centuries, and was a brewery in the seventeenth century. The mill was restored in the late 1980s by the council and as a working mill was a visitor attraction for a number of years. Financial constraints and the floods of 1997 have contributed to its closure, and its future remains uncertain.

The Brewery Bridge is one of ten bridges – pedestrian, vehicular and railway – which cross the River Lossie within the town. Now a footbridge, it spans the river adjacent to the cathedral. The view from the new road bridge to the east gives a splendid panorama of the old bridge, the east window of the cathedral and the restored chapter house. The Elgin Brewery, after which the bridge was named, was established in 1784. A fire in 1898 destroyed many of the buildings, but these were promptly rebuilt. In 1912 the property was bought for the town and the whole complex demolished to reveal the view of the cathedral from Newmill Road.

The Haugh, situated on the banks of the Lossie, was built in 1883 as the home of Alexander G. Allan, a prominent lawyer in the town. It saw service in both world wars when it provided accommodation for service personnel. The house was gifted to the town immediately after the Second World War by the then owner, Mrs H. C. Bibby, and was subsequently used as a pre-nursery training centre and music department for Elgin Academy. Having been sold and refurbished, The Haugh is now the Mansion House Hotel. The refurbishments, although extending the building, have preserved its character and architectural qualities.

THE TREE BRIG ELGIN

The Lossie meanders through the town and round the edge of Cooper Park on its way to the sea at Lossiemouth some seven miles away. There are a number of bridges and walks along the banks of the river, and the character of these walks has changed little since the days when this photograph of the 'Tree Brig' was taken.

MORAY STREET ELGIN

Moray Street, which runs roughly parallel with South Street and High Street, looking east. The tower on the left is that of the original town hall, opened in 1885 and alas destroyed by fire in 1939. Today it is the site of the police station. On the right is the 130-foot tower of the South Church. Its congregation was formed in 1843 following the Disruption and the church was opened in 1854. As a result of ecclesiastical unions in 1900 and 1929 it now belongs to the Church of Scotland and in the past year its congregation has been amalgamated with that of St Giles Parish Church.

Elgin from Town Hall, (looking W.)

Elgin's west end photographed from the tower of the old town hall. In the foreground are substantial houses in Gordon Street and Hay Street. West End Primary School, set up in 1875, is in the middle distance, with Forteath Avenue to its left and Mayne Road to the right. The dome and clock tower of Dr Gray's Hospital is on the right.

South College Street formed the eastern entrance to the town. This view has radically altered since the mid-1930s following the demolition of the buildings on the left and the widening of the street. When the relief road was built in the early 1980s the road was again widened and a large roundabout constructed here.

Dating from 1932, the Oakwood Rustic Motel was probably the first motel to be built in Scotland. Its wooden construction gave it a 'log cabin' look. Originally just a tearoom and petrol station, later additions included chalets, a wishing well, dance hall and lounge. Situated some two miles from the centre of Elgin, it was a favourite venue with people from the town. The lights atop the petrol pumps gave a flame effect. The Oakwood ceased trading in 1994, and is currently an antique and craft centre with a cafeteria.

THE CABINS, OAKWOOD RUSTIC HOTEL, NR. ELGIN.

A.4296.

The chalets attached to the Oakwood Rustic Motel were built around 1935. They probably reached the peak of their popularity during the years of the Second World War when many army, navy and RAF personnel were stationed in Moray. The chalets were finally demolished in the late 1980s.

CAFE, OAKWOOD RUSTIC MOTEL, ELGIN (11)

The interior of the café in the Oakwood Rustic Motel continued the log cabin effect of the exterior. It is back in operation today, serving as a café as part of an antique and craft centre.

HIGH STREET, ELGIN, LOOKING EAST 19

St Giles Church was built in 1827–1828, although there has been a church on this site since the twelfth century. The current building was designed by Archibald Simpson of Aberdeen in the manner of a Greek temple, with a superb portico of six fluted columns at the west end and a tower to the east. The tower is a copy of the choragic monument of Lysicrates in Athens.

HIGH STREET, ELGIN, LOOKING EAST.

10.

he area immediately in front of St Giles is known as the plain stones, and once served as a market place and feeing fair. The fountain, erected in 1846,
occupies the site of the old tolbooth which was used as the court room, council offices and town gaol.

HIGH STREET ELGIN.

A.4292.

High Street from the steps of St Giles. The war memorial was erected in 1921 to commemorate 461 men of the town who died in the First World War. It was designed by Percy Portsmouth of Edinburgh. The bronze figure holds a sword in its right hand as a symbol of victory and a torch in its left hand signifying peace. The base is made from local stone and has panels on the sides recording the names of the dead. To the right are the Assembly Rooms, built in 1822 but demolished in 1969. The Assembly Hall was a popular venue for dances and the building's demolition caused much controversy at the time. It was replaced by shops with office accommodation above.

High Street, Elgin (looking West)

Looking west along the High Street. Horse-drawn transport was the order of the day, and there isn't a car in sight. The businesses on the left include a flesher (butcher), boot and shoe shop and 'Mitchell's Economic Stores'.

HIGH STREET LOOKING EAST, ELGIN

D 1537

The fountain, built on the site of the old tolbooth, has not functioned as such for many years and is planted out each spring with annual flowers. This part of the High Street has now been pedestrianised. As part of the work connected with the pedestrianisation, water tanks were installed so that the fountain could once again be used, but it still remains dry. The ground floor of the former Gordon Arms Hotel now houses a drapery store.

24

Every high street had its branch of Lipton's, the place where many mothers went to do their daily grocery shopping. Butter would be cut from a large block and the bacon was sliced freshly to order, although the range of products was much smaller than the vast array that adorns the shelves of a modern supermarket. Nonetheless, service was far more personal. Hepworths, the well-known outfitters, stood next door to Lipton's. Its shop is now used by a branch of Next.

FORTEATH AVENUE, ELGIN

055

As Elgin expanded in the late 1800s, new houses such as these ones in Forteath Avenue were built. This has been described as one of the most picturesque streets in the town. It is made up of detached and semi-detached villas, each different from its neighbour, and adding to Elgin's rich architectural heritage.

South Street, Elgin

Along with High Street, Batchen Street and Commerce Street, South Street is Elgin's fourth main shopping street. This photograph, looking east, was taken from the corner of Batchen Street with Culbard Street leading off to the right in the middle distance. Today the building on the left houses the Imperial Bar, while the grocery and wine shop of Gordon McPhail, a long-established Elgin business, is to the right.

High Street looking west. In the foreground is the Little Cross, erected in the early fifteenth century by Alexander McDonald of the Isles as a penance for despoiling the cathedral. The cross – a 15 foot column on a plinth of four steps – is situated at what was the west entrance in the cathedral walls. This was a place of punishment, with stocks and a pair of leg irons in the vicinity. The top of the cross is formed by a sundial, the original of which was dated 1733, although this was replaced by a replica in 1941. The building with the three semicircular arches was originally a town house built for John Duncan and Margaret Innes in 1694, and later became Braco's banking house. Like many other Elgin buildings dating from the late 1600s it had an open arcade or piazza on the ground floor. This is one of the best surviving examples of this style of architecture.

Another view of Braco's banking house. Prior to the construction of the bypass road in the early 1980s, the entrance to Cooper Park led off to the left immediately beyond this building. Although originally built for John Duncan and Margaret Innes, it subsequently became the business premises of Duff of Dipple and Braco, an enterprising general merchant and moneylender of the north.

With the Season Greetings.

Museum & Little Cross, Elgin.

J.D.Yeadon,Elgin.

18B

This Italianate building, dating from 1843 and designed by Thomas MacKenzie, stands at what was the entrance to Cooper Park before the building of the bypass road. It houses the museum of the Moray Society, incorporating the Elgin and Morayshire Scientific Association, founded in 1836 to record and conserve the natural history, geology and archaeology of Morayshire. The collections, largely formed under the direction of the late Dr Duff and the late Rev. Dr Gordon, are numerous and have national importance. Until 1882 one of the smaller rooms was occupied by the Elgin Savings Bank. In 1896 the museum was extended by the addition of a rear hall and later a hall to the east of the tower. The tower provided accommodation on two floors for the custodian, and the top floor acted as an observatory. Recently the external stonework has been refurbished and the interior of the tower restored. The Moray Society remains very active to this day, supported by a grant from the Moray Council. Also in this photograph is the Little Cross with the trees of the Cooper Park in the background. The bypass now runs through this part of the park.

Valentine's Series
17213

The Muckle or Large Cross. In the Middle Ages the churchyard of St Giles served as a market place, and the market cross of Elgin, mentioned in historical records in 1365, probably stood within its bounds. In 1605 most of the churchyard's enclosing wall was removed to provide building material for the new tolbooth, and about 1630 a new cross was erected to the east of St Giles Church. Having been removed in 1792, it was re-erected in the same style in 1888 by Sidney Mitchell. The cross consists of a hexagonal platform with a classical column surmounted by the royal lion which had survived from the earlier structure. It was always known as the 'Muckle' Cross to distinguish it from the Little Cross further east on the High Street. The cross was once used for royal proclamations, but the internal platform now requires renovation, although the external stonework remains intact, if a little weathered.

EPISCOPAL CHAPEL, NORTH St. ELGIN.

The Episcopal Church of the Holy Trinity in North Street. This street was opened in 1821 but was cut in half when the bypass road was built in the 1980s; the church is in the north end of the former through street. Opened in 1826 and probably designed by William Robertson, it is one of a number of fine churches in Moray. Additions to the original building include a west wing built in 1875 and a commemorative porch in memory of Colonel Forteath of Newton, who gave his name to Forteath Avenue.

The church of Greyfriars dates back to 1409 and was probably built by Bishop John Innes. It formed the centre of an observantine monastery (of the Franciscan order). After the Reformation the buildings fell to the Crown and then to private owners. In 1891 the church was purchased by the Sisters of Mercy. They found the building too costly to maintain, but the then Marquis of Bute came to their rescue as a benefactor, commissioning the building's restoration in 1896. In September 1898 Mass was celebrated at the church for the first time since the Reformation. The complex remains the Convent of the Sisters of Mercy today.

Elgin has been blessed with very generous benefactors. Among these was Dr Alexander Gray, a native of the town who died in Calcutta in 1807. He left the princely sum of £20,000 for a hospital 'for the sick and the poor of the town and county of Elgin'. The foundation stone was laid in 1815 on the very day that news of the Battle of Waterloo reached the town. The building was designed by James Gillespie Graham and was opened in 1819. Its original mechanical clock ran until 1969 when it was converted to electric operation. Over the years the hospital has been developed and extended and in the 1990s underwent a major upgrading to become a full general hospital. Major building work was involved in this upgrading but the original frontage still stands guardian over the town. The fountain in the foreground was once removed to Cooper Park but has now been returned to its original position in front of the hospital.

Elgin Academy,

42B

I. D. Yeadon, Elgin.

This picture shows Elgin's second academy building, designed by A. & W. Reid to accommodate 350 pupils. It was opened in 1866 and superseded the original academy in Academy Street which had been built in 1801. The bell and gateway from the first building were re-erected in the grounds of the new school in 1906. Today this building has been incorporated into the campus of Moray College of Further Education. A new modern academy was built at Morriston. The building adjacent to the main academy building was Springfield House, a fee-paying school which was demolished when the college of further education took over.

STATION HOTEL. ELGIN.

The Station Hotel was built in 1853 for the Morayshire Railway Company. For a brief period it became the home of the Elgin Institute which provided education 'for the sons of the better classes'. Financial problems forced the closure of the institute and the building reverted to the Station Hotel. In the late 1950s it was renamed the Laich Moray Hotel, which remains a well-patronised hotel in the town to this day.

The Moray Floods of 1915
The G.N.S.R. Station, Elgin

The main station of the Great North of Scotland Railway. A schoolboy patiently awaits the non-arrival of his train, while the position of the signals appears to indicate no imminent change in the situation. The Morayshire Railway from Elgin to Lossiemouth opened in 1852, and in 1881 amalgamated with the Great North of Scotland Railway. This resulted in the opening of a further line into Elgin from Portsoy. The station in this photograph dates from 1902, and although it is no longer used for its original purpose the building has been retained and is used as a business centre.

Troop Train
Leaving Elgin Station

It is interesting to note that flooding didn't appear to stop this troop train departing from Elgin during the First World War. The trains of the 1990s were not so robust and were rendered unusable in the severe floods of 1997.

The Moray Floods of 1915

Arrival after the Flooding at Elgin

Friday 24 September 1915 was a warm and pleasant day, ideal for harvesting. Early the following day, however, a steady downpour began which continued uninterrupted until Sunday night. The River Lossie burst its banks in several places and the whole area from Elgin to Mosstowie was turned into a vast lake. Water at the railway station reached the level of the platforms. The situation was repeated 82 years later in July 1997 with the same disastrous results. When heavy rains cause the Lossie to burst its banks, other burns such as the Tyock Burn, which runs adjacent to the station lands, compound the problem. Not only is the main line flooded but the adjoining goods yards and fields are turned into a vast lake. Again this picture shows the ability of steam to forge its way through the floodwaters.

NICOL STREET, NEW ELGIN

As Elgin expanded away from the cramped living conditions of the closes off the High Street, so New Elgin began to develop on the south side of the town across the main railway line. New Elgin has expanded considerably over the years and continues to do so to accommodate the increasing demand for housing in the area.

GORDON STREET, NEW ELGIN

New Elgin was originally a village in its own right, separated from its larger neighbour by an area of marshland. Before the Second World War the council built some 56 houses in New Elgin, and since the war there has been a steady development of new houses. These well-built houses in Gordon Street look little different today, although the street is now full of cars.

MAIN STREET NEW ELGIN

New Elgin's main street forms part of the road south to Rothes and Aberlour. The houses are typical of the small cottage-type dwellings which were part of the original village, prior to its expansion. Although now incorporated into the Burgh of Elgin, New Elgin still retains its own identity. The shop still flourishes today, offering the same variety of goods as Mr James MacKenzie with the addition of a range of groceries.

The area known as Bishopmill is on the north side of the Lossie. The former Bishopmill primary school, in the middle distance, was established to serve the children of that area. By the 1930s larger school premises were needed and the current Bishopmill primary was opened in 1936. It was designed by the well-known local architect R. B. Pratt and was considered to be one of the finest educational establishments of its time.

Mr William Naughty was a rope spinner, born in Elgin in 1846. He lived at the Star Inn Close. This photograph was taken in 1890. Naughty, who was unmarried, died aged 46 as a result of a fire at his house on 3 April 1892 which appears to have been caused by an upset paraffin lamp. The newspapers of that day, namely *The Courier* and *Northern Scot* record the events of the fire and how Mr Naughty sustained serious burns to his face, hands and back. He was attended by Dr MacKenzie at the scene of the fire and later in the day was transferred to Gray's Hospital, where he died. Part of the building below Mr Naughty's house was used by Mr Henderson of the Star Inn as a beer cellar, and a newspaper report of the events of the fire recorded that 'below the ruins of the fire lie seven 36 gallon casks of beer and 18 gallon casks of porter'.

ADAM'S CHINA WAREHOUSE, ELGIN

John Adam's China and Glass Warehouse was located at 121 High Street. This picture, reproduced from a postcard, also appears as an advert in the *Northern Scot* Christmas edition of December 1915. John Adam was a native of Aberdeenshire who came to Elgin in his late twenties and succeeded in building up a large and profitable business as a retailer of glass, china and earthenware. He originally operated from premises in Batchen Street but moved to 121 High Street in January 1885. The advert which appears in the *Moray & Nairn Express* of January 1885 offers: 'Engraved spirit bottles and wine decanters from 1/6d per pair. Good cut and engraved tumblers and wine glasses from 3/- per dozen,' with the final line reading: 'Inspection respectfully invited'. John Adam served on the town council for a short period. He was also the oldest member of the Kilmolymock Lodge of Freemasons and Moray Golf Club.

Coronation Day School Procession.

A group of young ladies from the East End School, all rigged out in smocks and bonnets to celebrate the Coronation of Edward VII. The parade took place in the Cooper Park, which was given to the town in 1902 along with Grant Lodge (the latter became the public library). There is a fine array of ladies' fashions in this photo, and even the men have risen to the occasion with at least one straw boater in evidence. The East End School originated as part of the Elgin Institute, set up by Lieutenant General Andrew Anderson who endowed buildings in the east end of town 'for the support of old age and education of youth'. When the Education Acts of 1890 were passed the school ceased to be part of the Institute.

What appears to be a social gathering of the Elgin Labour Club in a field near the town. A rally in those days was somewhat simpler than the hype and jazz of a modern Labour convention.

Old House & Close, 41 High Street, Elgin.
Built 1685. Demolished 1911.

Old House & Clos, 41 High Street, Elgin.
Built 1685. Demolished 1911.

The arched thoroughfares through these buildings are described as closes, defined as a narrow alleyway or passageway leading into a small courtyard or enclosed space. Other terms such as vennel and wynd crop up to describe similar structures. A vennel is defined as a passageway between gable ends of houses (from the French *venelle*, meaning 'little street'). A wynd is a narrow street or lane at right angles to – or connected with – one or more main streets. The name Lossie Wynd is still in use today. Elgin High Street runs east-west and a number of interesting closes lead off the street. Over the years several have been demolished, but many have been preserved and restored. They have a variety of interesting names such as Harrow Inn Close, Cooperie Fraser's Close and Braco's Close.